THIS BELONGS TO me

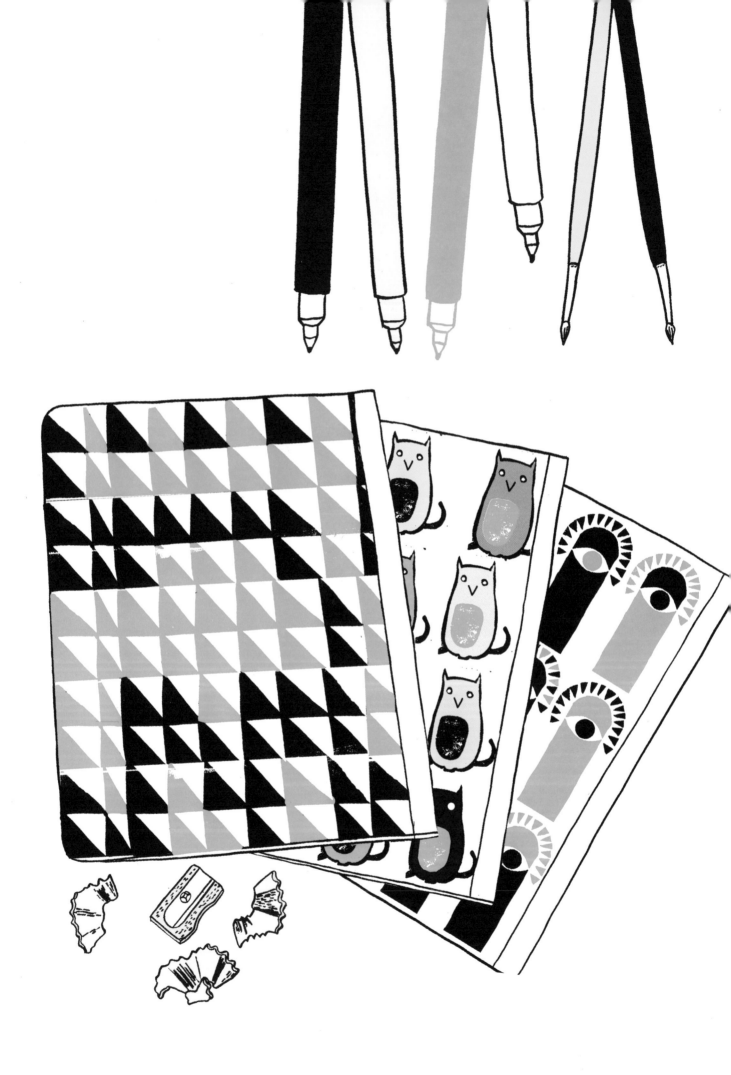

THiS BELONGS TO me

COOl WAYS TO PERSONALIZE YOUR STUFF

by Anna Wray

RP|KIDS

PHILADELPHIA • LONDON

First published in Great Britain by Ivy Press, 2013
First published in the United States by Running Press Book Publishers, 2013

Printed in China

ISBN 978-0-7624-4929-3

9 8 7 6 5 4 3 2

Digit on right indicates the number of this printing

This book was conceived, designed and produced by

Ivy Press

CREATIVE DIRECTOR Peter Bridgewater
COMMISSIONING EDITOR Georgia Amson-Bradshaw
MANAGING EDITOR Hazel Songhurst
EDITORS Melissa Fairley, Dereen Taylor
ART DIRECTOR Kevin Knight
DESIGNER Ginny Zeal
ILLUSTRATOR Anna Wray (additional artwork Venetia Dean)

Published by Running Press Kids
An Imprint of Running Press Book Publishers
A Member of the Perseus Books Group
2300 Chestnut Street
Philadelphia, PA 19103–4371

Visit us on the web!
www.runningpress.com

contents

No one wants their stuff to look plain and boring . . . Luckily, with the amazingly cool design projects in this book, it doesn't have to!

But before you go customizing crazy, there are just a few key things to keep in mind.

Always check with mom or dad before you tackle a project. You might think your walls are ready for renovating . . . but they might disagree!

For some projects, you need to iron, bake, or use a craft knife. You should always have adult supervision when using anything hot or sharp, and if you're really not confident about doing those parts, then ask a helpful adult to do them for you.

Make sure you carefully follow the manufacturer's instructions on dyes and glues to keep mess and danger to a minimum (always a good idea!). Along the same lines, it's really important to protect yourself and the area you are working in, so have old clothes,

Running Stitch: Here's how . . .

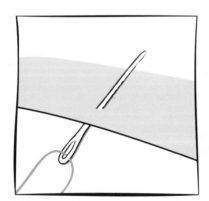

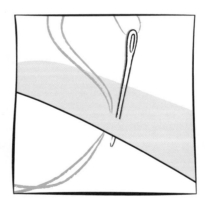

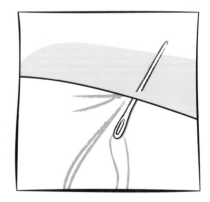

1 Thread your needle and tie a knot at the end. Begin sewing by poking your needle up through the fabric.

2 Poke the needle back down through the fabric next to where you just came up and pull the thread down into your first stitch.

3 Now poke your needle back up through the fabric, leaving a small space from the previous stitch. Then poke the needle back down through the fabric again, making your second stitch.

sheets, and newspapers handy for the messier projects. Don't panic; some projects are reassuringly big on style and small on mess!

To focus on awesome ideas, instead of awesome skills, tricky techniques have been kept to a minimum. One thing you may need to master is a simple running stich (see below if you're not yet "up and running" on that!).

When you are excited and inspired by the many customizing opportunities around you, remember to take your time and not rush the creative flow. In some cases, the end results are permanent—but thankfully that's not the case concerning Trendy Body Art!

It's time to pick a project and get creative!

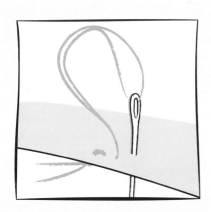

4 And just keep on running, making sure you leave the same size space between each stitch to get an even row of stitches.

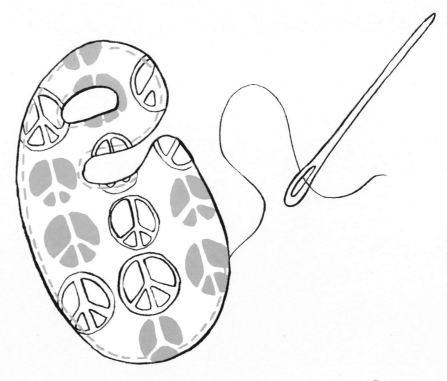

Clothes

Doodle Sneakers

Let the world see your art by taking it for a walk.

Plain, canvas sneakers can be boring, but it's really easy to jazz them up. All you need to do is doodle.

Unlike traditional artwork, doodles are quick sketches, scribbles, or illustrations that pop into your head in an instant. They can be shapes, cartoons, letters, patterns, or a mix of all of these things. It's a fun way to draw because there are no rules—anything goes!

You might want to try doodling some . . .

Funny Faces

Abstract patterns

Words or phrases

FreeStyle Space

Before you doodle on your sneakers, try out some designs on these blank templates first.

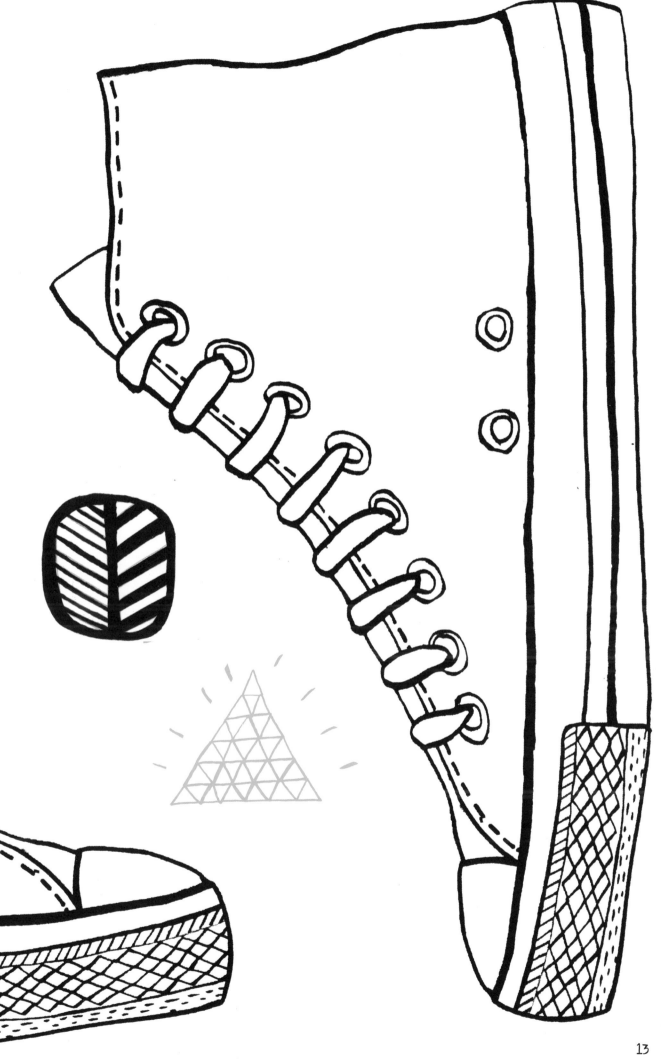

You'll need...

- Plain canvas shoes
- Hard pencil
- Eraser
- Square paintbrush
- Round paintbrush
- Fabric paint
- Permanent marker pens
- Waterproofing spray
- Colored or patterned laces (optional)

Snazz Up Your Sneakers

Now that you've practiced your doodles, you can follow these easy steps to make your fantastic footwear.

Don't forget to decorate the shoe tongue.

1 Use a hard pencil (a No. 4 is good) to draw your favorite doodles directly onto the first shoe. Draw lightly in case you make a mistake and need to erase it.

2 Do the same on the other shoe. You can repeat the same design or try something new. Take your time because the finished look depends on what you do at this stage.

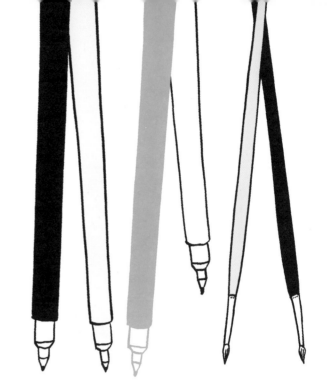

3 Choose your fabric paint and color in the larger areas, using a flat square brush. Try not to cover the pencil lines, because you will be going over these later with a marker pen.

4 Let your shoes dry to avoid smudging your designs.

Put your shoes next to a heating vent to dry or, if it's sunny, leave them outside. Don't move on to Step 5 until the fabric paint is dry.

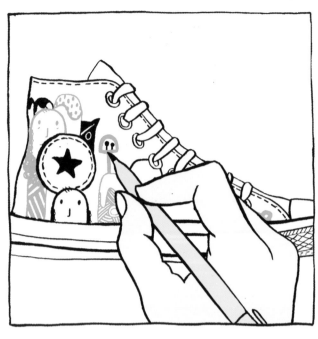

5 When the fabric paint is dry, use a permanent marker to draw over the pencil lines.

6 Check your shoes carefully. Have you missed any areas? Are there any gaps around the marker outlines?

Read the spray instructions.

Shoe laces come in a lot of colors and patterns. Pick a pair that goes with your trendy new designs.

7 When your shoes are dry, spray them with waterproofing spray. You can buy this from most shoe stores. It will protect your designs. Swap the plain white laces for some colored or patterned ones, if you prefer!

Once you've laced your snazzy sneakers, meet up with your friends to show off your designs. Just watch out for muddy puddles on the way!

Top Tip!

You can use your doodle designs again. Try using them to decorate a T-shirt.

Graffiti Jeans

Graffiti is an art form that originated on the streets, so it's the ideal inspiration for edgy streetwise fashion.

The jeans on this page have a graffiti-inspired image on the back pocket, and because the design is white, it will go with any outfit—perfect!

Customizing jeans isn't a new concept for the fashion industry, but this project will show you how to do it at home.

Think of some motifs you could use for your designs . . .

Freestyle Space

**Try out your
ideas here.**

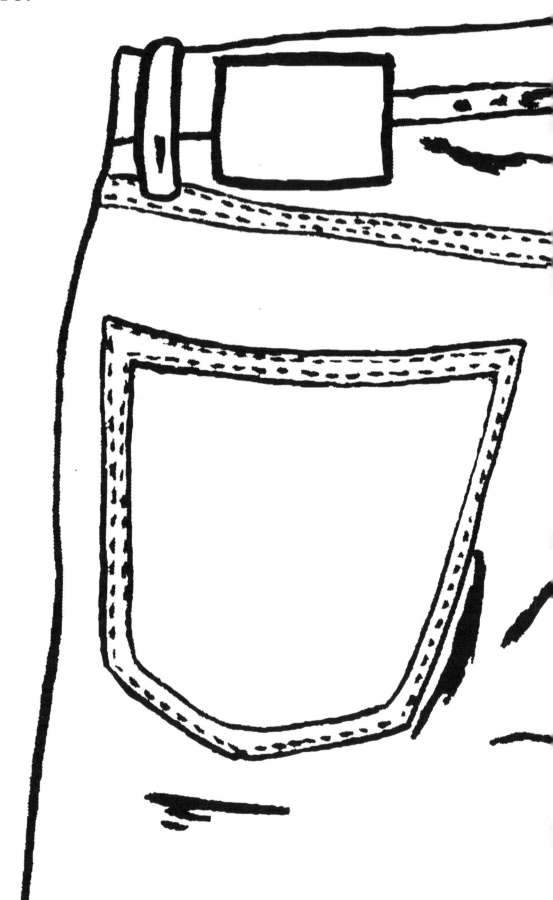

You'll need...

- Jeans (washed and ironed)
- White dressmaker's marking pencil
- Assortment of paintbrushes
- White fabric paint
- Iron

Dead Cool Denim

Once you've decided on your design, follow these easy steps to create your own pair of unique jeans.

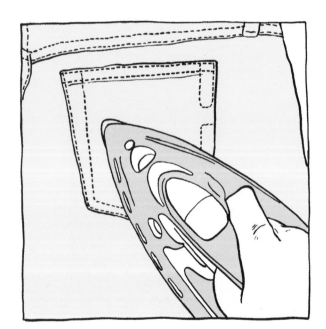

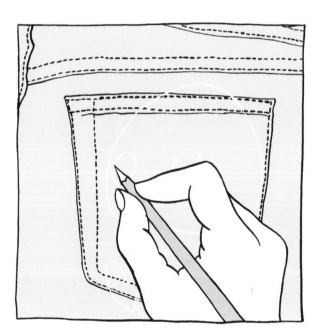

1 Make sure your jeans are washed and ironed (ask an adult to help if you aren't used to ironing), especially the back pockets, which are the areas you are going to paint.

2 You can either draw your design right on your jeans or make a cardboard template to draw around (tracing paper won't work here).

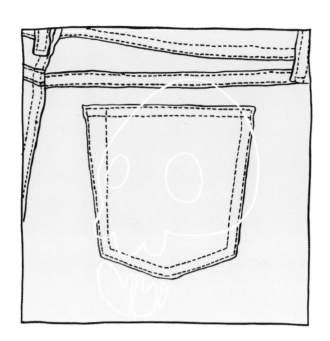

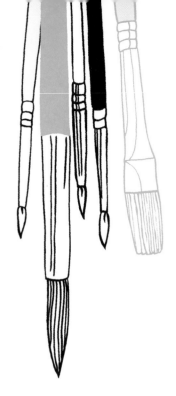

3 For a more dramatic effect, you might want to place your design so it overlaps the back pocket.

4 Use a fine-tip paintbrush to outline white fabric paint around the edges and details of your design.

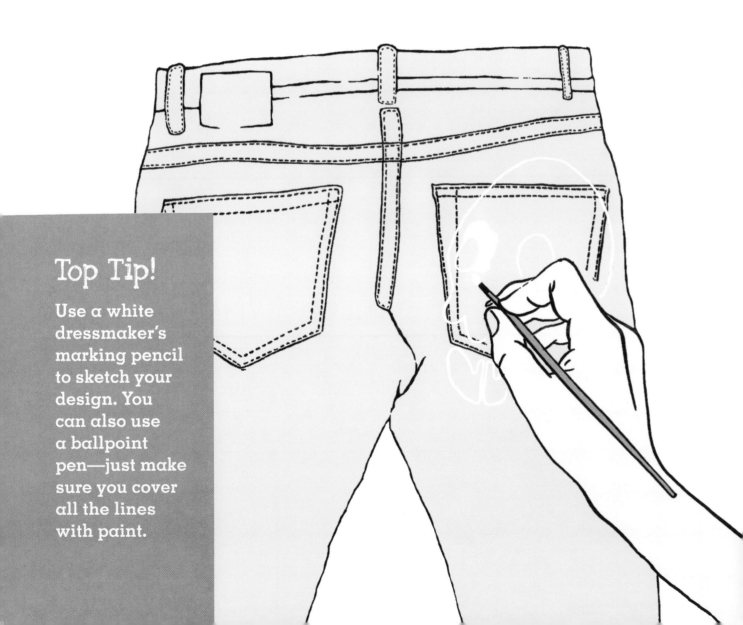

Top Tip!

Use a white dressmaker's marking pencil to sketch your design. You can also use a ballpoint pen—just make sure you cover all the lines with paint.

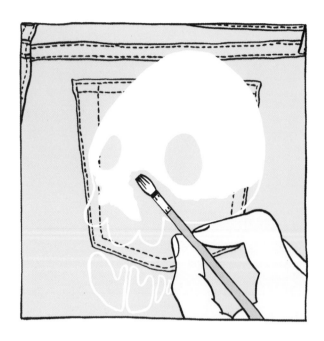

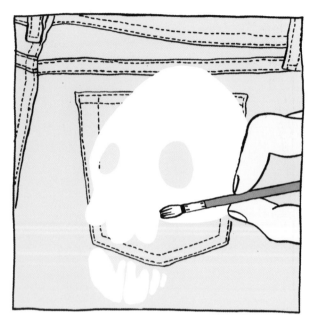

5 Once the paint is dry, use a thicker brush to paint inside the design outline, and then let this dry.

6 If it doesn't look thick enough, give your design another coat of paint; just repeat the process.

You can design motifs of your favorite things or look at some magazines for the latest trends.

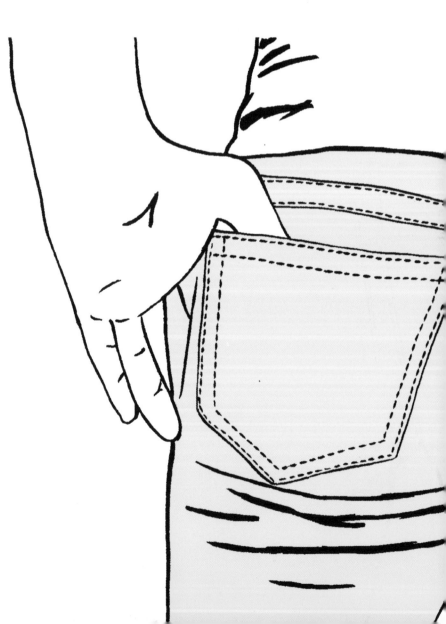

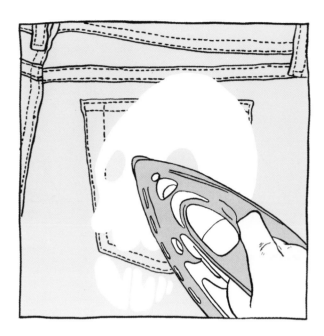

7 Follow the instructions on the fabric paint packaging and seal your design by ironing over it. Ask an adult to help with this if you need to.

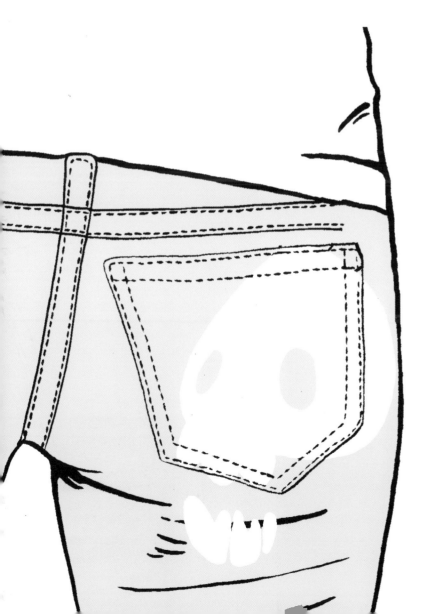

Bar Code T-Shirt

Masking tape is an art and design staple.

It won't leave a sticky residue and peels off easily. This makes it ideal for masking areas for painting, as well as taping art paper to boards and walls. But there is another more exciting use for masking tape: you can use it to create striking T-shirts, such as this cool bar code design.

Coded for coolness!

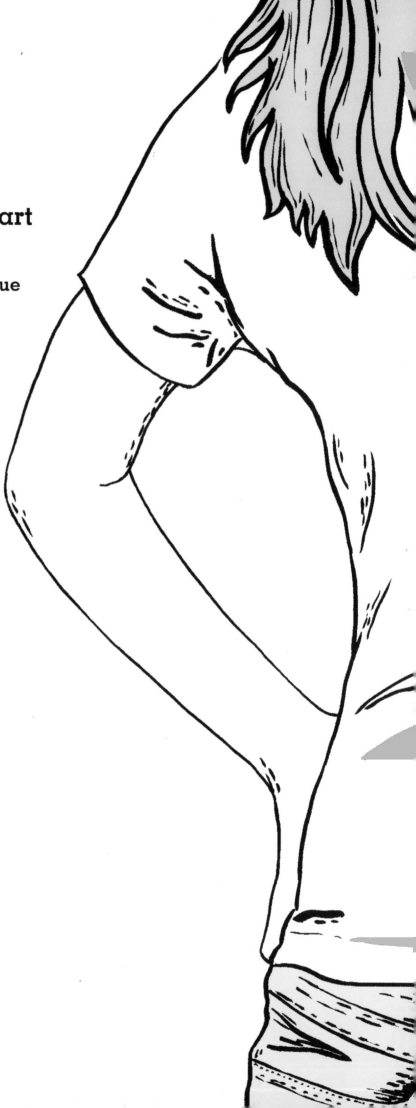

FreeStyle Space

Practice using masking tape to make sure your bar code design is nice and neat.

Tape-tastic Tee!

Once you're confident using the masking tape, follow these steps to make your own bar code T-shirt.

Try to cut very straight lines.

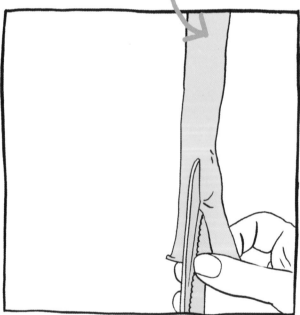

1 Put your ironed T-shirt on a flat surface and use the masking tape to make a rectangle on the front.

2 Cut lengthwise along strips of masking tape with scissors to create neat, straight bars. Cut some bars wide and others narrow.

3 Use the strips of tape to create the vertical bars inside the rectangle. Make sure the gaps between them are different sizes, just like a bar code. You can lay them out freehand or use a ruler to measure them.

4 Review your pattern and redo any sections you think need improving. Remember that the spaces between the masking tape will be the painted areas.

Top Tip!

Use masking tape to create typography by using the same technique.

5 Pour some black fabric paint into a plastic cup and carefully paint over all the spaces between the masking tape bars.

6 Let the T-shirt dry.

7 Once the T-shirt is dry, peel off the masking tape and follow the ironing instructions on the fabric paint packaging to seal your design.

Top Tip!

Use a few colors in your design to turn your bar code into modern art.

Try not to set off
any cool-ometer scanners
when you go shopping
with your friends!

Easy Embroidered Lettering Hoodie

Appliqué is a technique used in the fashion industry to add texture, pattern, and visual interest to clothing.

This next project will turn your ordinary hooded sweatshirt into an individual fashion statement— a one-of-a-kind designer piece.

Give hoodies a chance!

FreeStyle Space

What do you want
to say? Choose your
message or statement
and try it out here.

You'll need...

- Hooded sweatshirt (washed)
- Pencil
- Tracing paper
- Paper-backed fusible webbing (such as Wonder Under®)
- 8 x 10-inch remnant of plain or patterned fabric
- Iron
- Scissors
- Needle and thread
- Sewing machine (optional)

Word Up Your Hoodie

Now that you've practiced your slogans, you can follow these steps to create your own appliqué hoodie.

1 Draw your chunky lettering by hand. Or, to create a design like this, use a funky font on your computer and print your word in the right size, using a word processor such as Microsoft Word—see the Top Tips box for more information on how to do this.

2 Print out the lettering and then trace over it on some tracing paper, using a pencil.

Top Tip!

This design was created using a groovy 70s-style font called Bell Bottom Laser from dafont.com; it was enlarged in Microsoft Word to make a bigger template.

3 Now iron the paper-backed fusible webbing onto the piece of fabric you want your letters to be made from. Follow the instructions on the webbing packaging and ask an adult for help if you find it difficult.

4 Trace the lettering onto the webbing backing, making sure the letters are the right way up. To check this, take your tracing paper with the pencil-traced letters upside, and mark it UPSIDE. Then turn it over and trace again on the other side of the letters.

Write UPSIDE here.

5 Use your pencil to scribble over the traced letters on the UPSIDE. This will transfer the lettering onto the webbing backing.

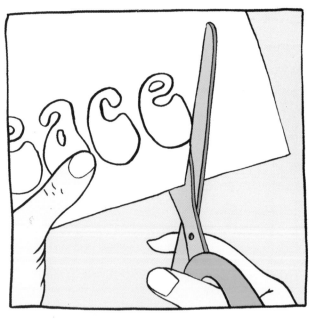

6 Cut each letter out of the fusible webbing, using scissors. Peel off the paper backing and arrange the letters on the hoodie. Iron the letters to make them stick; if they move too much, you may need to pin them first.

7 Use a contrasting colored thread to hand stitch a neat running stitch around the letters, or ask an adult to help you use a sewing machine.

8 Sew about $1/8$ inch from the edge of the letters, keeping your stitches evenly spaced. You can use thicker thread for a chunkier look.

Top Tip!
You can cut
each letter out
of a different
pattern or color.

AcceSSorieS

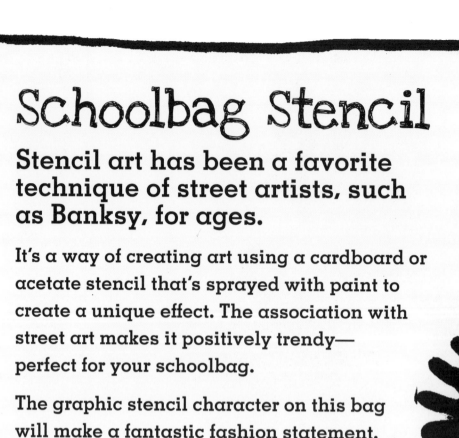

Schoolbag Stencil

Stencil art has been a favorite technique of street artists, such as Banksy, for ages.

It's a way of creating art using a cardboard or acetate stencil that's sprayed with paint to create a unique effect. The association with street art makes it positively trendy— perfect for your schoolbag.

The graphic stencil character on this bag will make a fantastic fashion statement.

Turn your bag into a work of art!

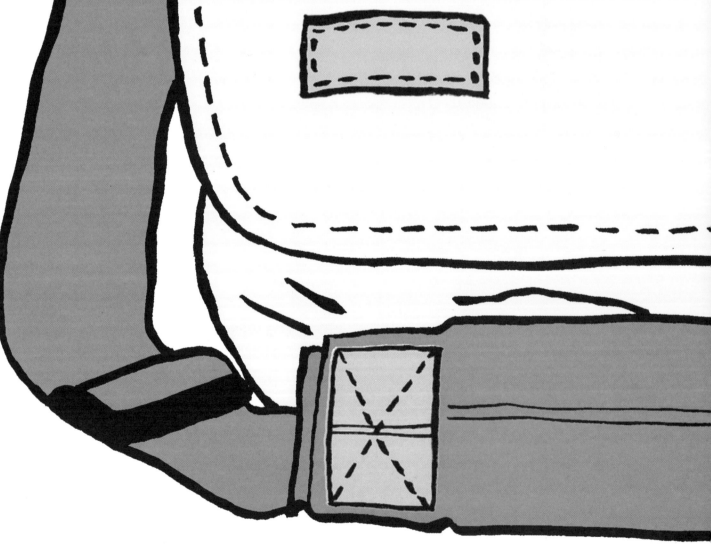

FreeStyle Space

Get creative and design your own stencil template.

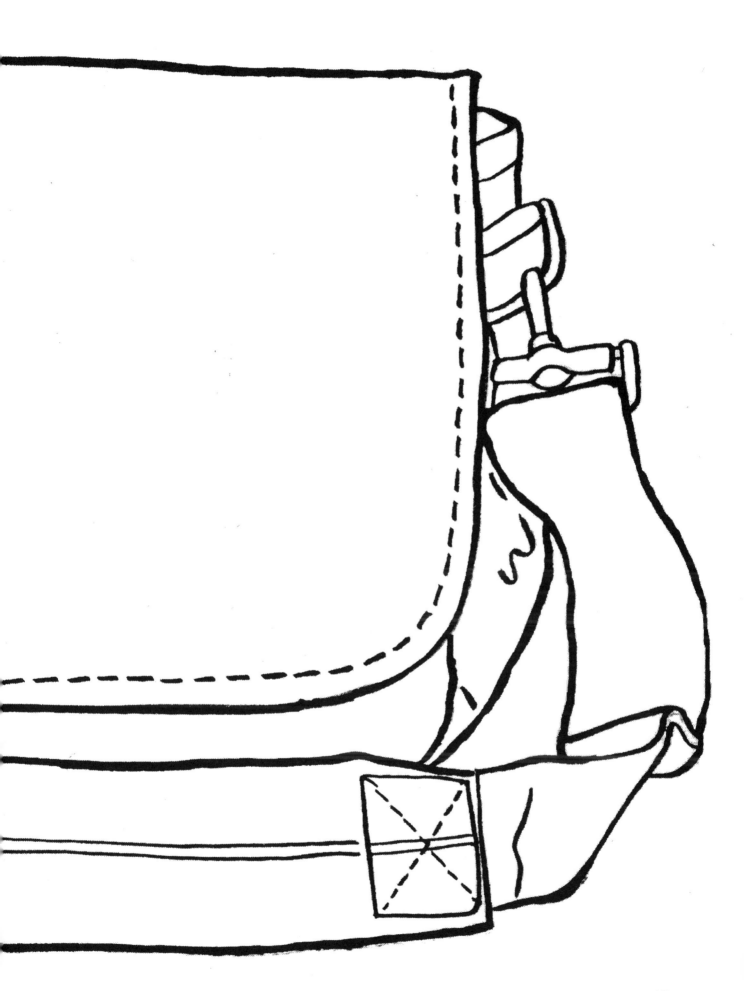

Street School Style

Use your own designs and follow these steps to create stylish stencil art.

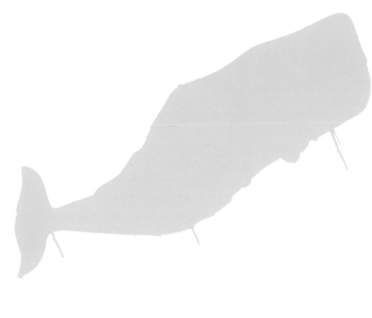

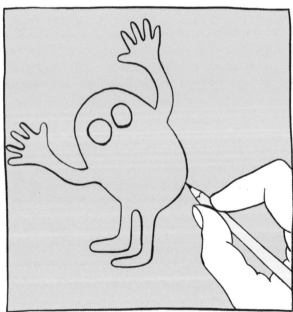

1 Draw your character design on the cardboard using a pencil, so you can erase any mistakes. Leave a wide border around the character.

Top Tip!

Don't limit yourself to a schoolbag; this would work just as well on a T-shirt, using fabric spray paint.

2 Place the cardboard on a cutting mat and use a craft knife to cut it out; alternatively, you can use scissors. The eyes will be taped to the bag individually before spraying, so don't throw them away.

3 Choose the area where you want your design to go. Make sure it's as flat as possible. Use masking tape to attach the edges of the template to the bag. Now hold the eyes in place with double-sided adhesive tape.

Make sure your design isn't too fragile or thin. It needs to hold together when you cut it out. Use your craft knife with care!

4 Cover the rest of the bag so the spray paint doesn't get all over it.

5 Spray over your stencil, making sure you don't miss any spots.

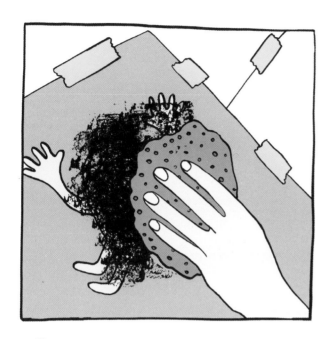

Top Tip!

You can add a second color to your design by creating another cardboard stencil that overlays the first. This character could have red boots, for example.

6 Alternatively, you can use fabric paint and a sponge, and press it evenly over the stencil. Make sure the paint isn't too thin.

7 Once you've finished spraying, remove the template and let your design dry. Then enjoy showing it off to your envious friends!

Practice using spray paint on newspaper before you spray your bag.

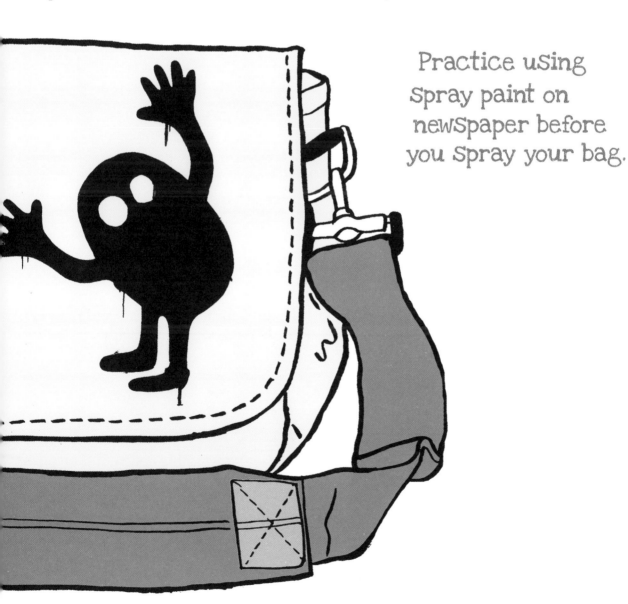

Customized Headphones

Polymer clay (such as Fimo®) is a colored modeling material that is easy to use and ideal for making amazing minature sculptures.

With the recent boom in crafting, modeling has become a popular art form. You can create a lot of things in 3-D: jewelry, ornaments, charms, figures, or anything else you can imagine.

Polymer clay is perfect for modeling because it's readily available from most art supply stores and it's inexpensive. There really isn't anything to keep you from going wild with this stuff!

Become a top model (model maker, that is).

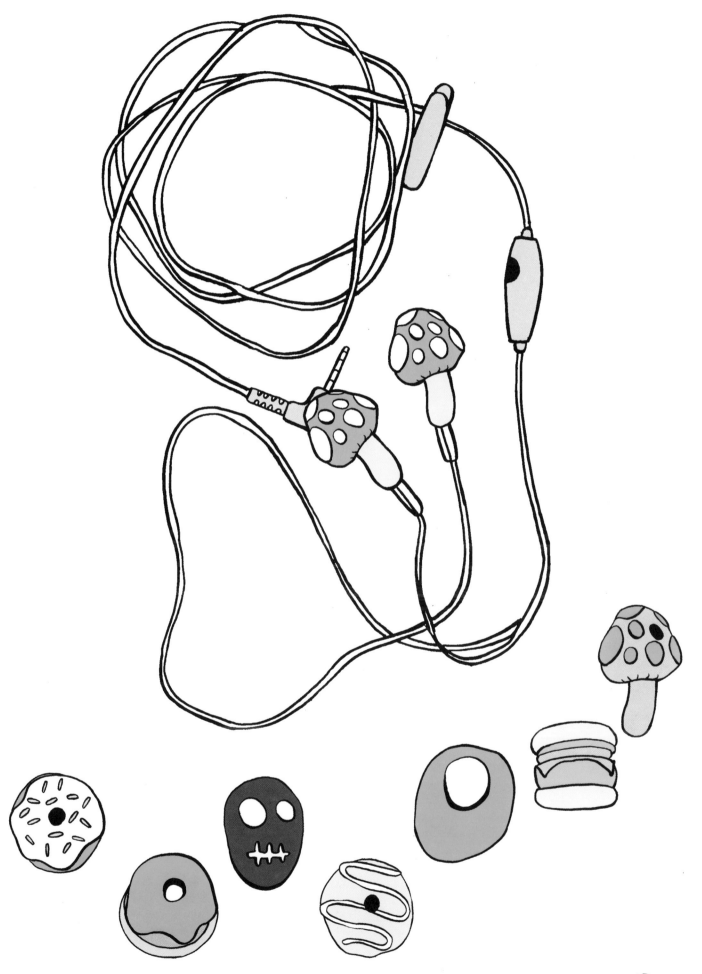

FreeStyle Space

Customize your
headphones with
clay models. Try out
some designs here.

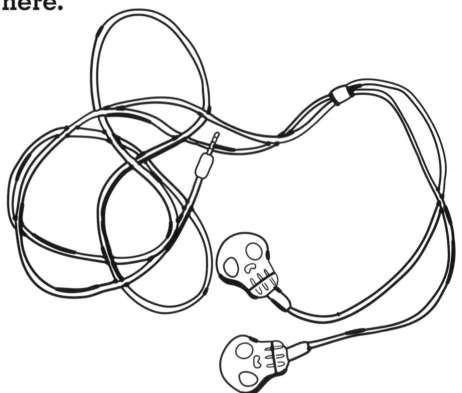

You'll need...

- Polymer clay (three colors: light brown for the base, blue for the icing, and white for the sprinkles)
- The end of a fine paint brush (or a match)
- Headphones
- Knife
- Superglue

Polymer Clay Doughnuts

Follow these steps to create your own miniature doughnut headphones. They're a sweet treat for your ears!

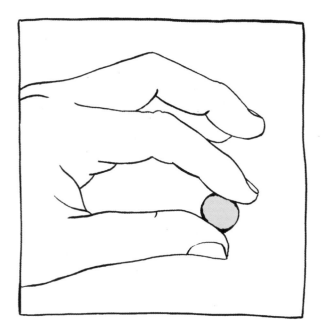

1 Take a small piece of light brown clay (about the width of one of your headphones) and roll it into a ball between your palms. This will be the doughnut base.

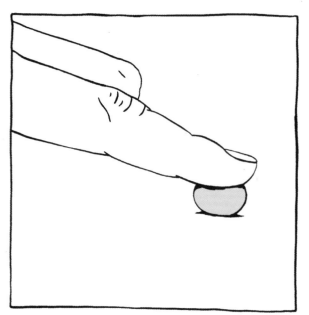

2 Gently squash the ball with your thumb onto a clean surface to make a doughnut shape. Hold it against one of your headphones to be sure it's the right size.

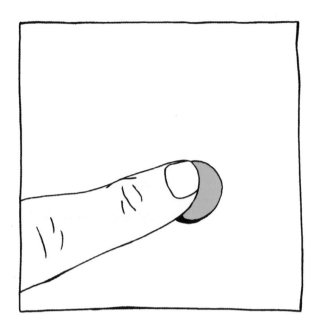

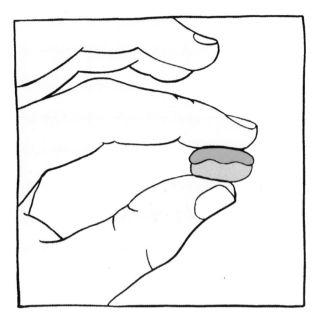

3 To make the icing, take a smaller piece of blue clay and roll into a ball, but this time squash it more firmly, so it's just a fraction of an inch thick.

4 Gently press the icing onto your doughnut base, so the icing covers just half of the edge around the doughnut. Smooth it down.

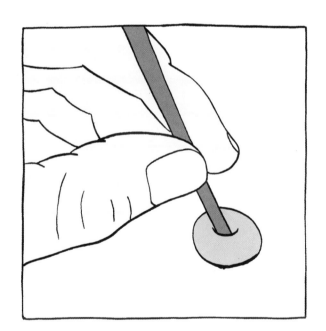

Always remember to
check the position
and shape of your model
against your headphones.

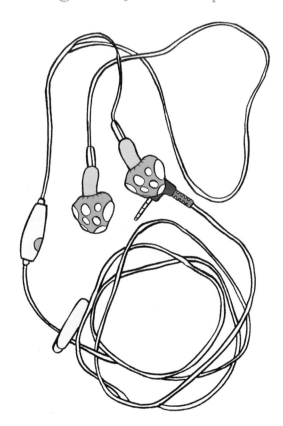

5 Use the end of a fine paintbrush to push a hole through the middle of the doughnut and wiggle it until you're happy with the size. Then press the model gently onto the back of a headphone, so it takes on some of its shape. This will help with gluing later.

6 Remove the model from the headphone and make the sprinkles by rolling the white clay into a very thin snake (thin enough to resemble tiny sprinkles). Use a knife to chop off little sections and add them to your doughnut with the end of a pencil.

7 Now follow the instructions on the clay packaging to bake your doughnut models. Ask an adult to help if you are not used to using the oven.

It's best to ask an adult to help you when you're using superglue.

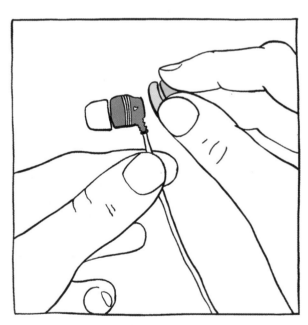

8 Apply superglue to the backs of your headphones and position the baked, cooled doughnuts.

Top Tip!

For a glossy finish, you can paint your models with polymer clay varnish.

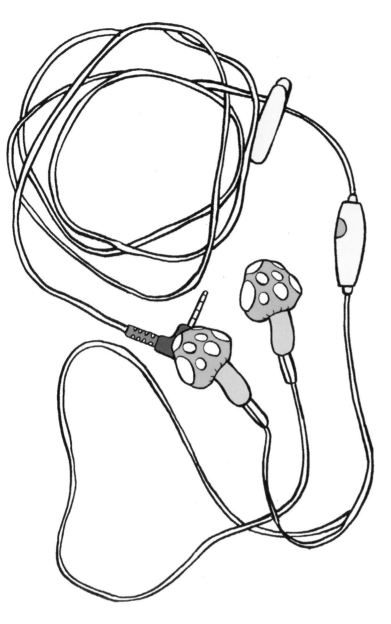

Top Tip!

You can make scary eyeballs for Halloween using a similar technique.

Customized headphones make great gifts for your friends and family.

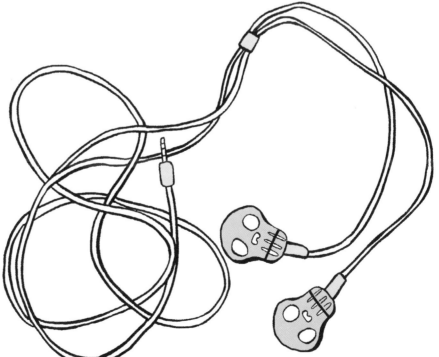

59

Temporary Retro Sailor Tattoo

Temporary tattoos are terrific because you can have fun with fashion without the downside of having a design on your skin for the rest of your life (not so cool).

This project shows you how to apply a tattoo that looks 100 percent real, using jagua, which is a totally harmless extract of the fruit *Genipa americana*. It's been used for body ornamentation in South America for centuries.

If an anchor tattoo isn't for you, try something else instead.

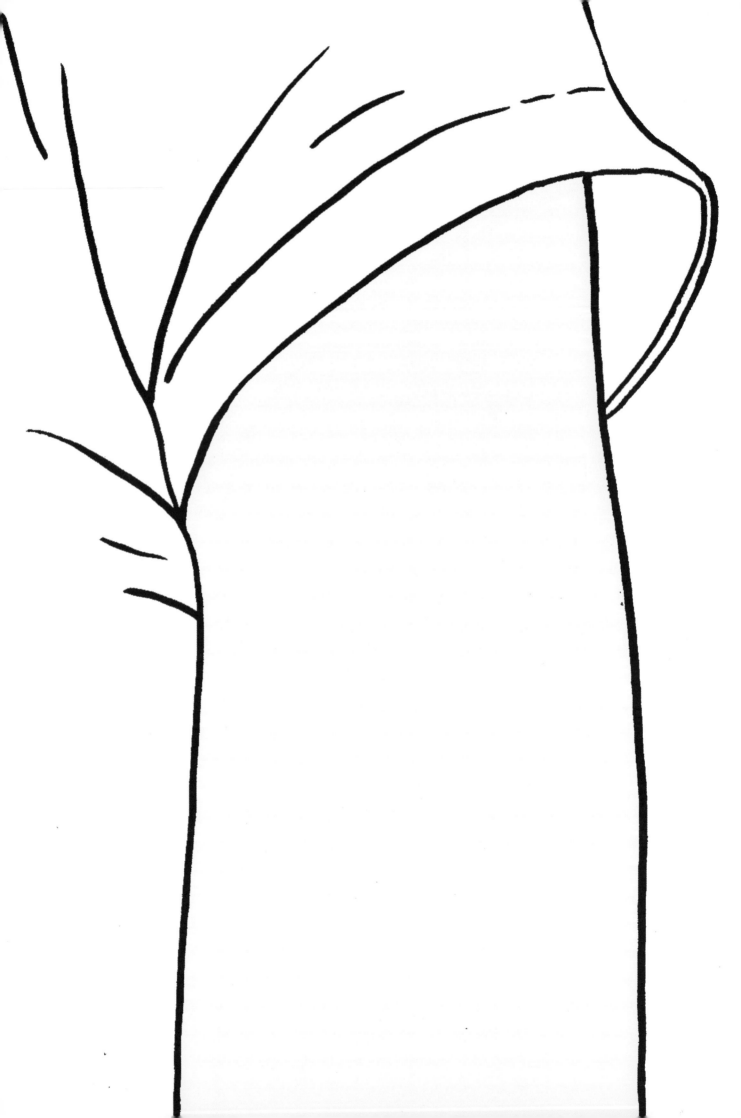

Freestyle Space

Try out some tattoo designs here. How about a butterfly or a shooting star?

You'll need...

- Eyeliner pencil
- Jagua temporary tattoo ink (a natural fruit-based dye)
- Fine paintbrush

Trendy Body Art

In just a few easy steps, you can have a temporary tattoo. You can buy jagua from many online craft supply stores.

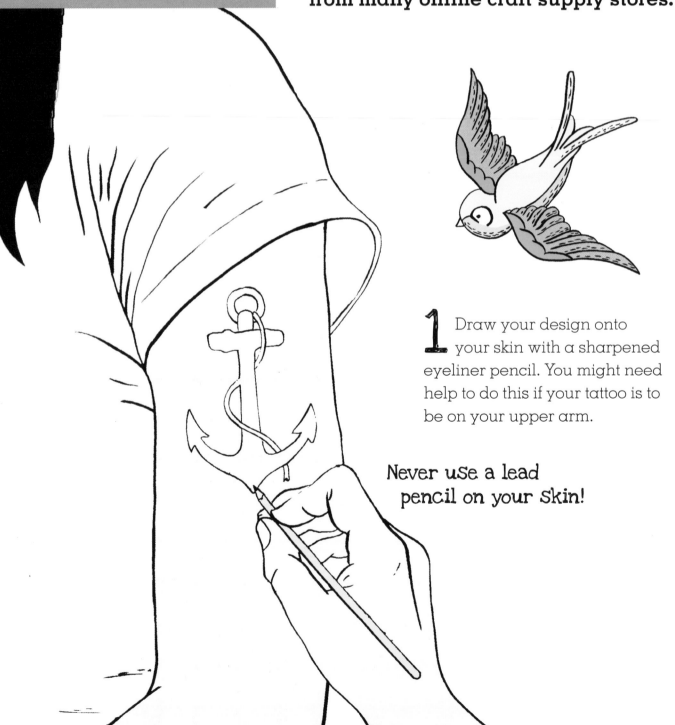

1 Draw your design onto your skin with a sharpened eyeliner pencil. You might need help to do this if your tattoo is to be on your upper arm.

Never use a lead pencil on your skin!

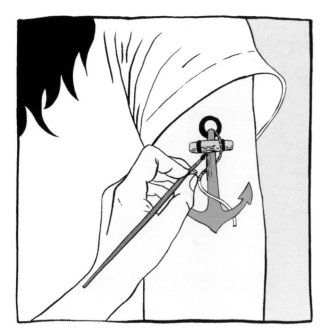

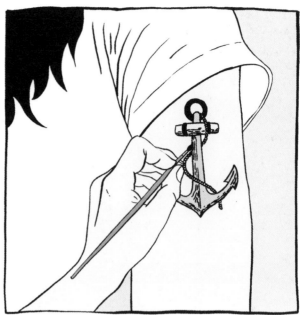

2 Load a fine brush with jagua and apply the paint liberally over the eyeliner pencil lines. The paint should sit in a raised pool on top of the skin.

3 Once you have applied a layer of jagua, immediately add another to make sure the paint is thick enough and completely covers your design.

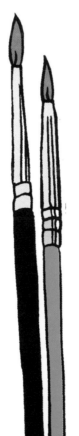

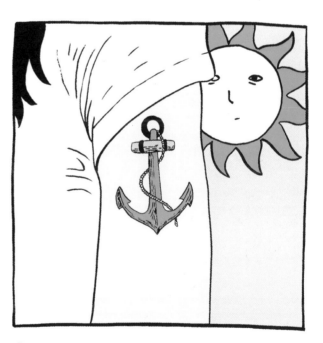

Top Tip!

Use Henna if you can't get hold of jagua. It works just as well.

4 The paint will be dry to the touch in ten to thirty minutes, but it should stay on the skin for two hours to get the best results. Be sure to keep the design uncovered.

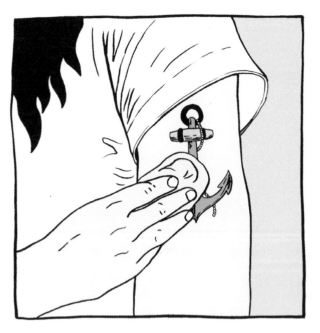

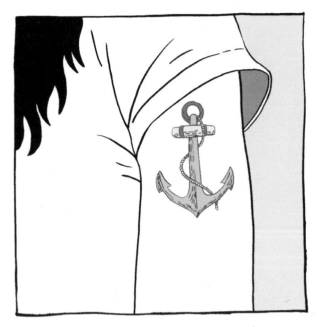

5 After two hours have passed, wash the tattoo with cool water.

6 The tattoo will be very pale at first. It takes two days to properly develop and darken.

7 Your new tattoo should last ten to fifteen days. It will fade over time after that, but if you want it to last longer, just paint jagua over the existing design.

Why not set up your own tattoo parlor and invite your friends for a makeover?

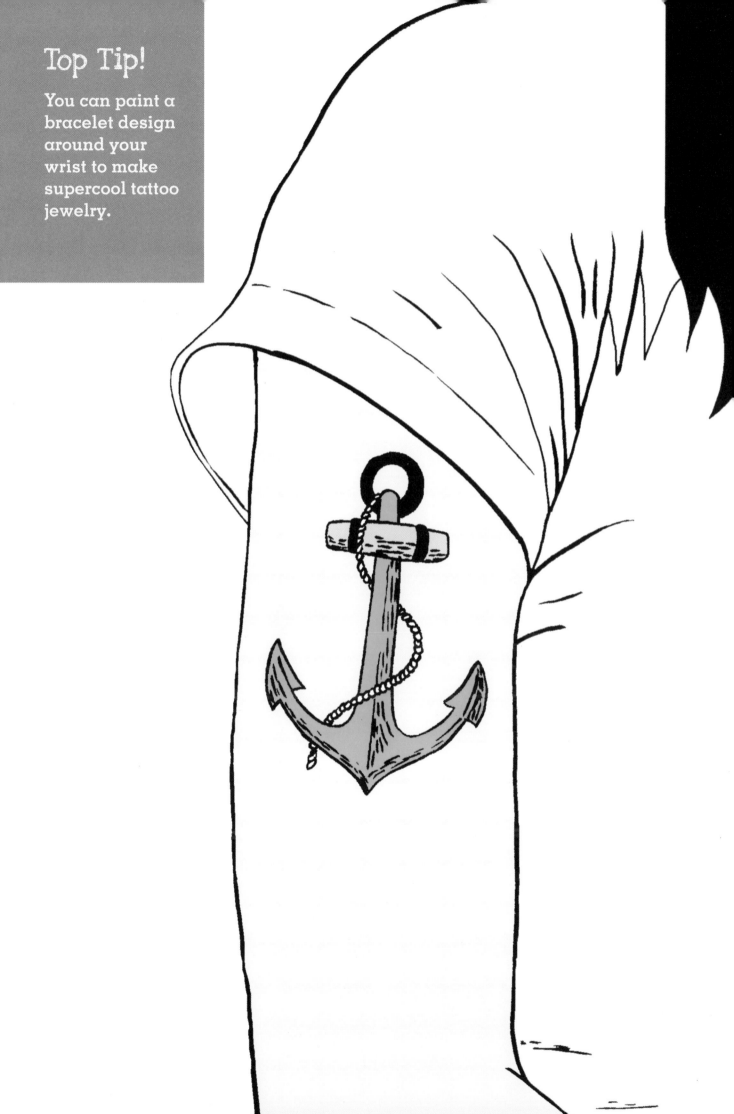

Top Tip!

You can paint a bracelet design around your wrist to make supercool tattoo jewelry.

Abstract Stamp Pattern Notebook

Repeating patterns are a great way to turn a boring notebook or sketch pad into an eye-catching item.

Using a 6 x 8-inch piece of linoleum, this project shows you how to make simple triangle stamps that, when repeated, will make wonderful multicolored geometric designs.

Don't be a square, make some triangles!

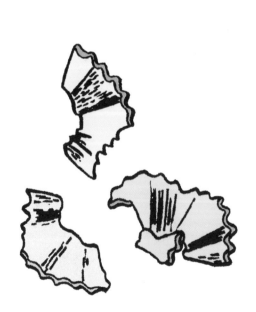

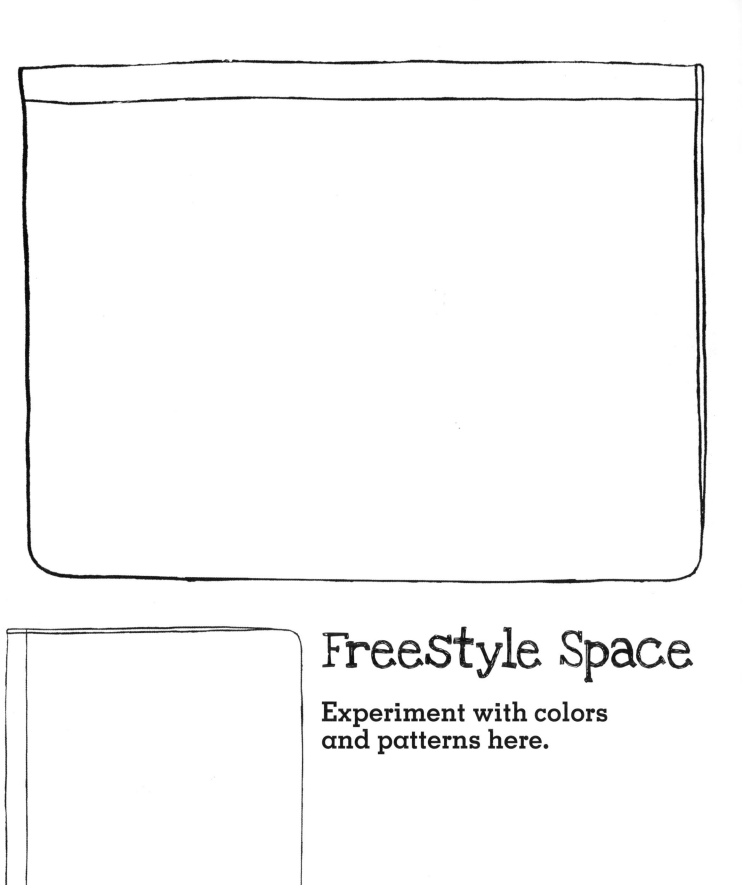

FreeStyle Space

**Experiment with colors
and patterns here.**

Perfect Patterns

Once you've experimented with repeating geometric patterns, try following these steps to create a pattern using linoleum and ink.

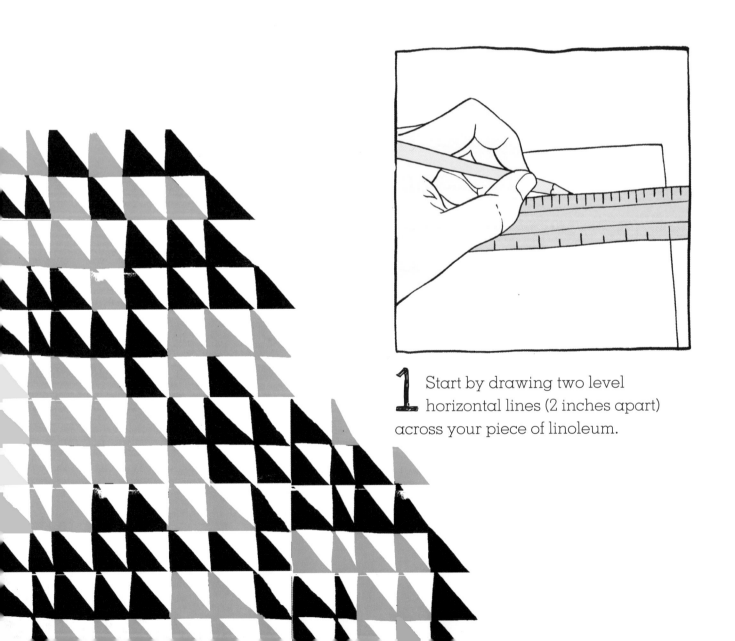

1 Start by drawing two level horizontal lines (2 inches apart) across your piece of linoleum.

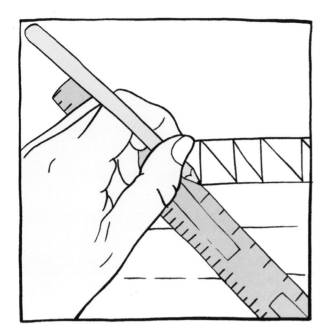

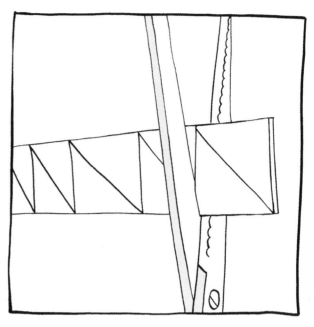

2 Use the horizontal lines as a guide to make sure your triangles are all the same depth. In this pattern, the triangles are all different angles to add to the kooky effect.

3 Once you are happy with your triangles, choose five or six and carefully cut them out, using a strong pair of scissors.

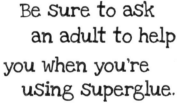

Be sure to ask an adult to help you when you're using superglue.

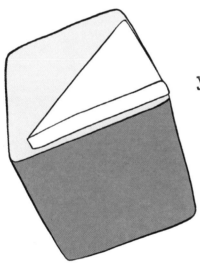

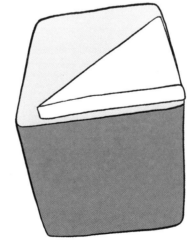

4 Now you have five or six random-sized triangles, but they are all the same depth. Attach them to your wooden blocks, using superglue.

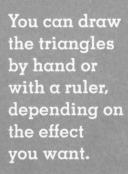

Top Tip!

You can draw the triangles by hand or with a ruler, depending on the effect you want.

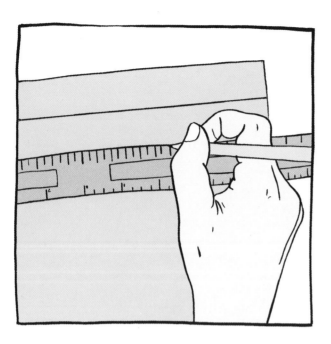

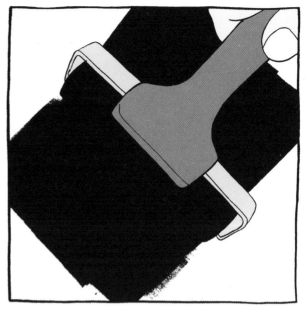

5 Draw two horizontal lines on your book cover (2 inches apart), just as you did before in Step 1.

6 Use your roller to roll the printing ink onto a flat surface. Roll the ink for a few minutes to loosen it up.

7 Press the linoleum block stamp into the ink and practice on another surface so that you get the consistency right.

8 Stamp alternate rows using the different triangle shapes. Experiment with various colors and combinations and let dry.

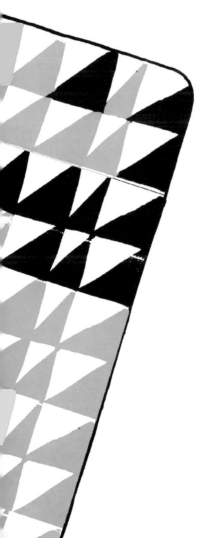

Use a linoleum cutter to make different shapes and icons on your linoleum blocks. Ask an adult to help!

Top Tip!

You can make a repeating pattern out of any design you choose. For more elaborate designs, such as simple icons, carve each stamp using a linoleum cutter, so you can cut more accurately.

Linoleum Block Card Printing

The linoleum block-printing technique has been around since the beginning of the nineteenth century. It's a popular and easy way of making unique handmade prints.

You don't need any specialized equipment—just a few basic tools—and the result is a very unique look that is much richer than anything you can buy in the store. Once you've designed your printing block, you can repeat the pattern as many times as you like.

Try some funky images on your printing block.

Freestyle Space

Design a character who would look good on a greeting cards.

You'll need...

- 8 x 11-inch piece of soft linoleum
- Pencil
- Eraser
- Linoleum cutter
- Water-soluble block printing ink
- Brayer (little roller)
- Cardboard

Crafty Creative Cards

Now that you have your design, follow these easy steps to create your own linoleum block prints.

Don't make the designs too detailed. Keep them simple.

1 Draw your design in pencil on a piece of linoleum. Make sure that the design isn't too small.

2 Use an eraser to make corrections before beginning to cut. Remember that the final printed image will be in reverse, so do any writing backward.

3 Now use the linoleum cutter to shave away the area around your image. You are carving your design, instead of cutting it out, so don't push all the way through the linoleum. Keep in mind that the raised surface (the uncarved area) will be the part that prints.

Remember not to cut too deeply!

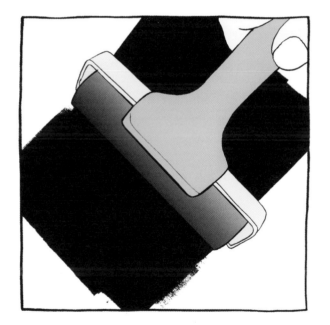

4 Use your roller to roll the printing ink onto a flat surface. Roll the ink for a few minutes to loosen it up.

Top Tip!

Take care when using the linoleum cutter! Always push away from your body and push forward instead of down. It's a good idea to first practice on a spare piece of linoleum!

5 Then roll the ink directly onto your linoleum block image, making sure the block is completely covered.

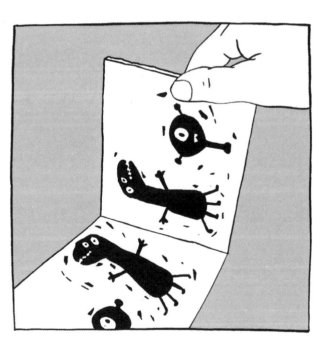

6 Press your image onto a piece of cardboard and place a heavy book on top and press down.

Fasten a piece of string across your window to dry your prints in the sunshine.

Top Tip!

Create a two-color design by cutting a separate linoleum block for the second color.

7 Remove the linoleum block. If the image isn't dark enough, just add another layer of ink onto your block. Then let your print dry.

Room

Vinyl Wall Stickers

Vinyl wall decorations are a popular way to customize bedroom walls, but you don't have to shop around for the perfect sticker because you can make it yourself!

Vinyl is a clear plastic-base material with an adhesive backing, so it's ideal for creating simple wall designs with a bold graphic look.

Design a fake window vinyl sticker for your wall and create your own view.

FreeStyle Space

What would you like to see on your bedroom walls?

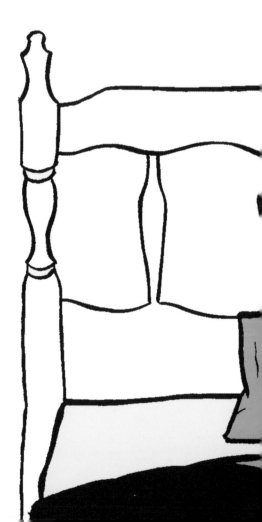

You'll need...

- Paper
- Pencils (including a No. 2)
- Thin cardboard
- Sharp small scissors
- Sticky tack
- 9 x 12-inch clear, self-adhesive vinyl in one or more colors (you can order this from art supply stores)
- Eraser

Super Stickers

Once you've chosen your design, it's time to create some stunning stickers to brighten up your bedroom.

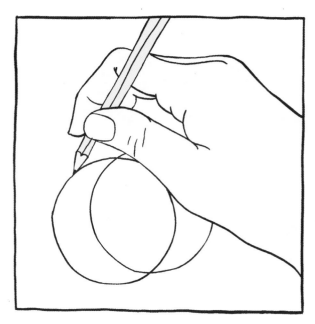

1 First practice drawing your design on paper. Think carefully about how it will look. Will it be easy to cut and glue? Keep your shapes bold with as little fine detail as possible.

2 Draw your design in pencil on a piece of cardboard. This will be the cutting template for your vinyl sticker. Draw around objects if you need help getting your shapes right.

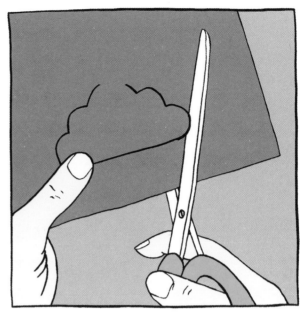

3 You can use several colors in your design. The clouds here are blue vinyl and the tree trunk is black vinyl. Smaller vinyl stickers can be used together to create a larger design.

4 Now cut out your cardboard template, using sharp scissors. Try to cut as neatly and carefully as possible.

Try out your design by attaching your card template on the wall with sticky tack.

Top Tip!

Vinyl stickers also look cool on the back of a laptop or any other similar surface.

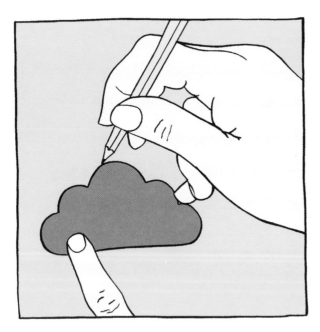

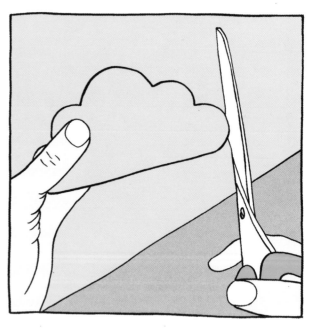

5 When you are happy with your template, place it on the vinyl. Hold it firmly in place and draw around it with a soft pencil (such as a no. 2). This outline will be erased later.

6 Carefully cut out your design. Don't rush this part. When you are done, erase any pencil marks on the final vinyl design.

Vinyl comes in sheets or rolls. You can get it from art supply stores or order it on the internet.

Top Tip!

There is nothing to keep you from using three, four, or more colors of vinyl in your designs.

7 Draw fine pencil marks on the wall as a guide for placing the vinyl. Peel the backing off the vinyl sticker and smooth it onto the wall.

Use your hand to smooth out any bubbles in the sticker. Rubbing it with a square piece of cardboard also works well.

Batik Curtains

Batik means "dye with wax," and is a traditional art form originating in Indonesia in Southeast Asia.

A batik design is a repeated pattern that can be as simple or complicated as you want it to be. It's the perfect way to transform plain, boring curtains—simply add your own wonderful border.

Freestyle Space

Get started on drawing your curtains. Literally.

You'll need...

- Curtains (muslin, cotton, or linen work best)
- Pencil
- Beeswax
- Saucepan
- Bowl
- Pot for holding the melted wax
- Thin paintbrush
- Dye
- Large container to use as a "dye bath"
- Old newspapers
- Iron

Cool Curtains

With some paint and dye, you can create curtains with style. Just follow the steps.

Top Tip!

It's important to have clean curtains, because dust and stains may affect how the dye is absorbed by the fabric.

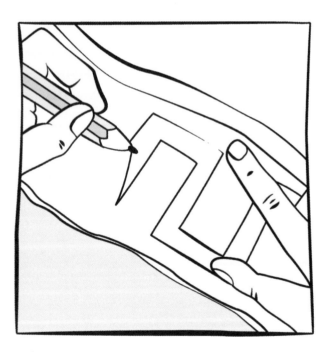

1 Draw your design onto the curtain fabric with a pencil.

Warning!
You need an adult to help you when you are working with hot wax!

Top Tip!

Remember to paint the wax where you DON'T want the design to go!

2 Carefully melt the wax in a double boiler (the same way you would melt chocolate). The wax needs to be hot, but not boiling, around 350°F.

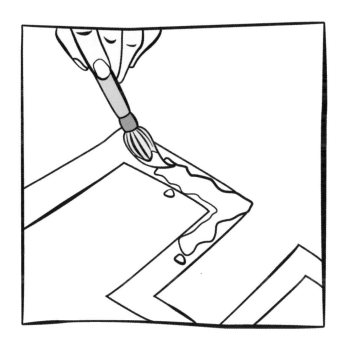

3 Pour some of the hot wax into a pot. Then paint your design, using a small brush. You'll need to work quickly, before the wax cools down. If the wax doesn't soak into the fabric, it needs to be hotter.

4 Let the wax dry. If you are eager to move on to the next stage, put the curtains in a bag in the freezer to speed up the drying process.

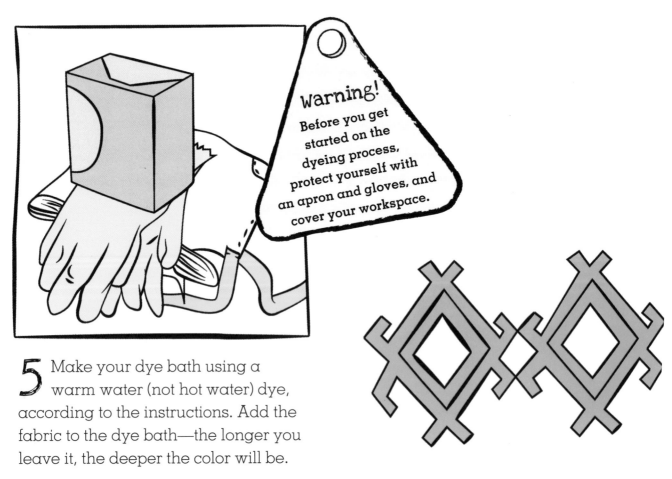

Warning!
Before you get started on the dyeing process, protect yourself with an apron and gloves, and cover your workspace.

5 Make your dye bath using a warm water (not hot water) dye, according to the instructions. Add the fabric to the dye bath—the longer you leave it, the deeper the color will be.

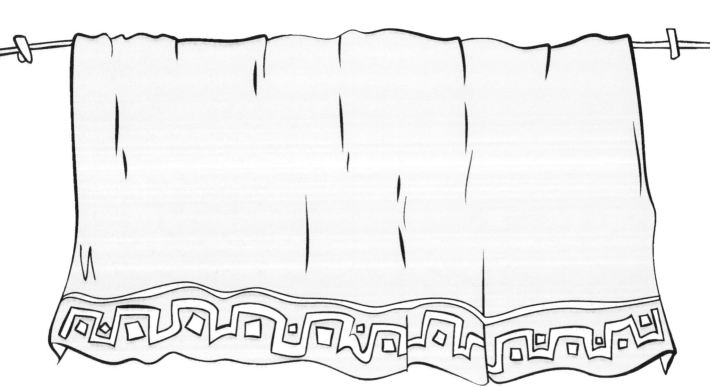

6 Rinse your fabric following the instructions on the dye packaging and let dry.

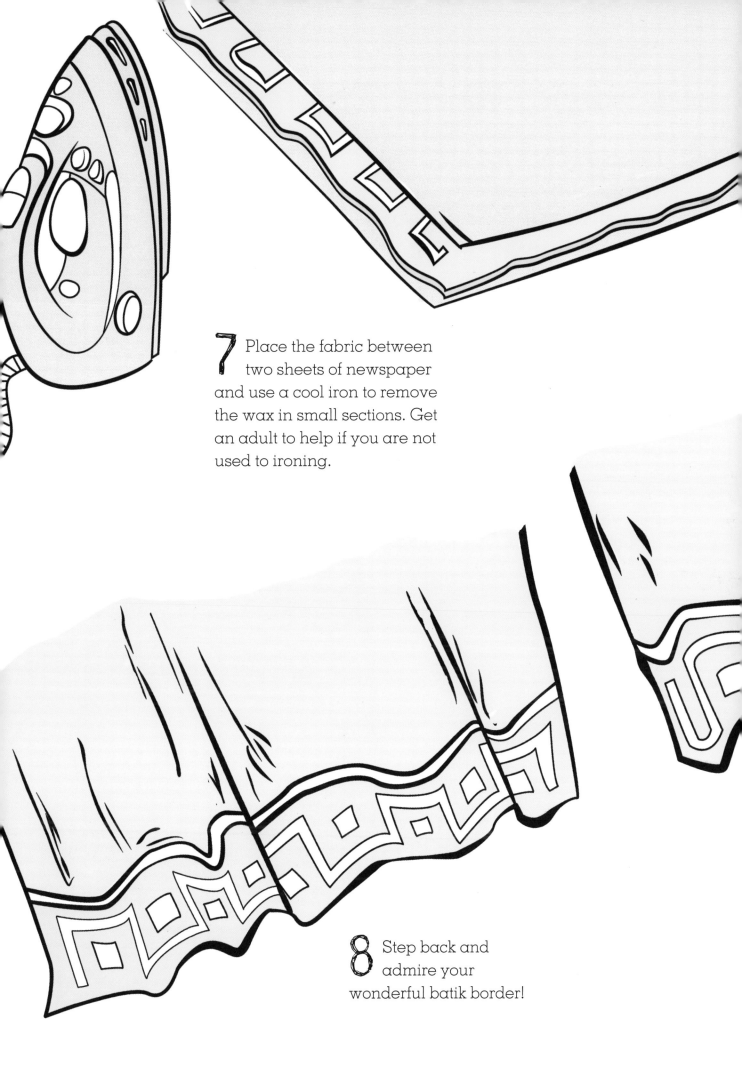

7 Place the fabric between two sheets of newspaper and use a cool iron to remove the wax in small sections. Get an adult to help if you are not used to ironing.

8 Step back and admire your wonderful batik border!

Comic Book Tabletop

Collage is a form of art where separate images are arranged and glued to a backing.

Collage is a popular technique with many artists and designers who use pictures from magazines, newspapers, and other printed sources to create many types of artwork.

This project will show you how to create a tabletop collage, perfect for revamping a boring bedroom.

Tabletops that pop!

Freestyle Space

Redesign this dull tabletop.

You'll need...

- Loads of images
- Scissors
- Tabletop
- Multipurpose glue
- Paintbrush
- Old cup for glue
- Clear, matte acrylic varnish spray

Tabletop Trendsetter

First choose your images and then start creating. Follow the easy steps to make your cool collage.

1 Take some time to collect great images. They might be retro comics found at a book fair, old photographs, patterned wrapping paper, or pictures from magazines.

2 Make sure the tabletop you choose is smooth and dust free—and that it's not an heirloom! You should check with an adult first.

3 Once the tabletop is clean, start cutting out the images. Think about varying the size of your imagery to create a more dynamic composition.

Consider using black-and-white images and then add splashes of color here and there.

Top Tip!

You can cover a box or pencil case using the same collage techniques.

4 Arrange the images on the table. Make sure you like the way they all fit together. Try mixing it up by layering the images on top of each other.

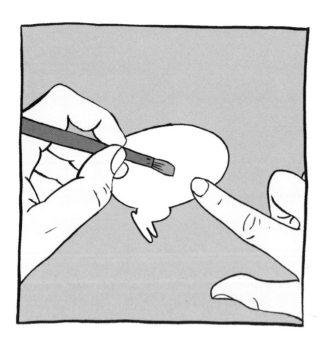

5 Pour some multipurpose glue into an old cup and make sure your brush is the right size for the job. Then start gluing the undersides of your images and placing them on the table.

6 Gradually build up the design. Always make sure you press down the corners and edges so that they don't catch and peel off over time.

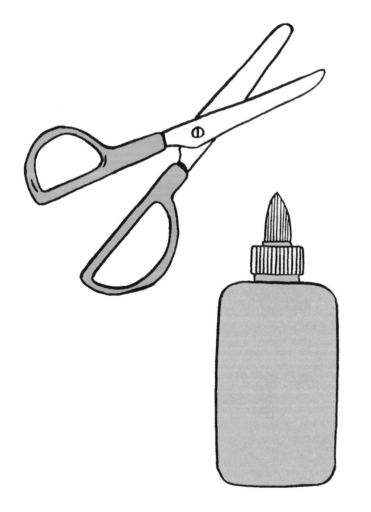

7 Let the collage dry, and then finish the tabletop with three coats of acrylic matte varnish. This will make the tabletop durable and waterproof.

Top Tip!

Varnish the table outside, or in a well-ventilated room. Let it dry between coats.

If you don't have any suitable furniture, you can make collage artwork to hang on your wall instead.

Abstract Art on the Bed

Have you ever noticed that a plain white bedsheet is almost exactly the same size and proportion as a very large art canvas?

So it makes sense to turn a plain bedsheet into the most amazing abstract bedspread painting. It will completely transform the look and feel of your bedroom; people will wonder if they've just walked into an art gallery. And you can add to this project by transforming your pillow cases, too.

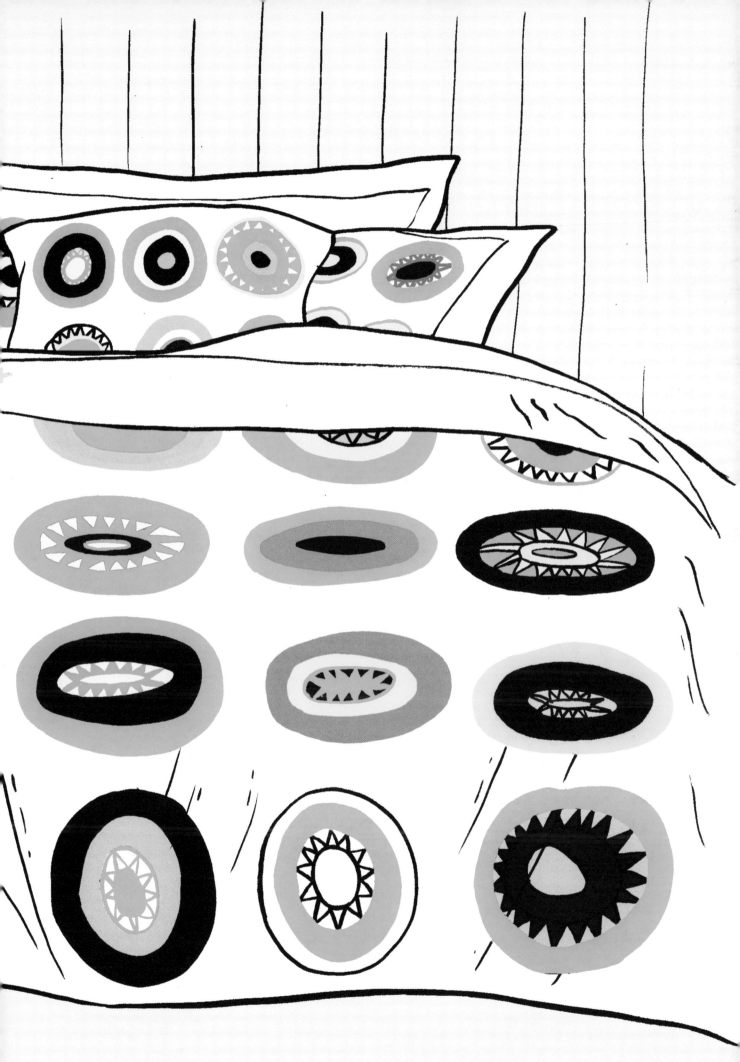

Freestyle Space

Create the coolest designer bedspread and some art you can sleep in.

Bedspread Chic

Once you've chosen your bedspread design, follow these easy steps to create your own bedroom art installation.

1 Find an area in your house or garage to tape your sheet to the wall or the floor, using duct tape. You will need a stepladder to tape your sheet to the top of the wall.

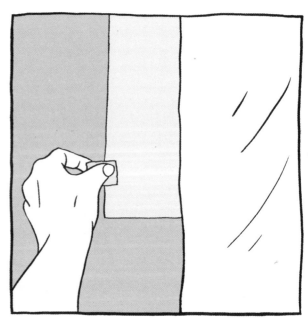

2 Tape some newspaper around the edges of the bedsheet to protect the wall or floor from paint. Make sure you put newspaper underneath the sheet as well.

3 Now pick a color and paint thick outlines of big circles about 2 inches apart. You can always first draw the outlines in pencil.

4 Once you've finished the first set of circles, pick a different color and paint thinner circles inside the thick outer circles.

You can pick colors that complement each other or you can choose ones that clash to shake things up.

Top Tip!

If you are short on space, you can paint only your pillow cases.

5 Paint a third set of circles inside the other two sets. Alternate the thickness again—mixing up the circle widths and colors will make it more interesting.

6 Paint patterns between the circles to add more detail and contrast. Use the ½ inch-wide paintbrush to paint this additional detail.

Once your new bedspread
is done, make a sign
for your room saying:
ART GALLERY OPEN!

7 Once you are happy with the pattern, let it dry and then follow the instructions on the paint packaging to set the design with a hot iron. Ask an adult to help if you are not used to ironing.

Top Tip!

Don't worry if your circles are slightly untidy, because the design is meant to look abstract and spontaneous.

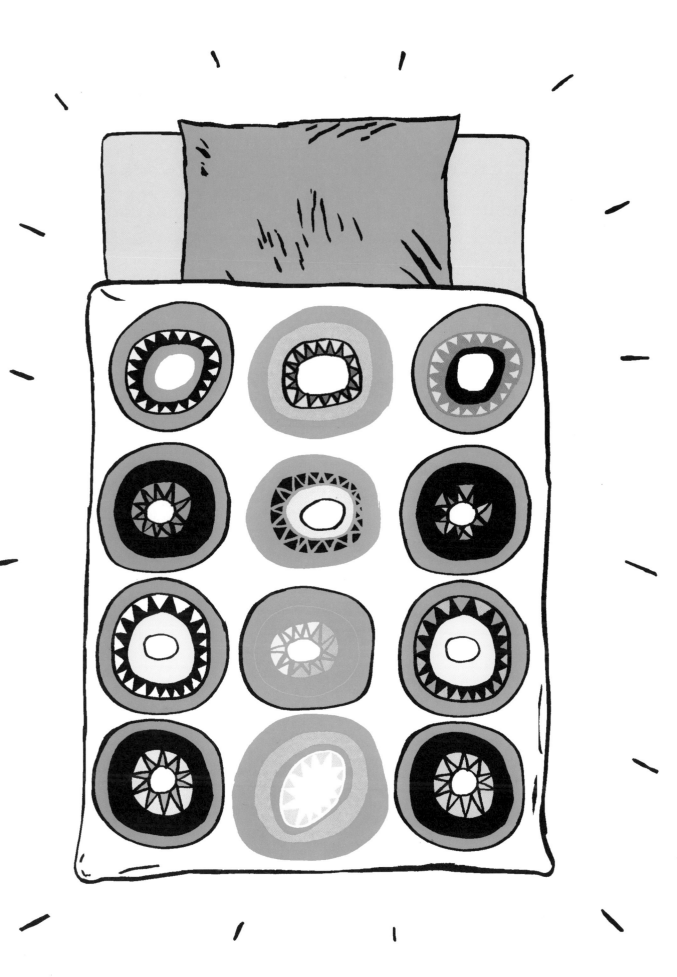

Illustrated Lampshade

Why have a plain beige lampshade when you could have one covered with colorful birds or a crazy abstract pattern?

Fortunately, this last project will banish boring beige shades and replace them with your own fantastic designs. You'll find out how to create a unique atmosphere in your room and make your lampshade a real work of art.

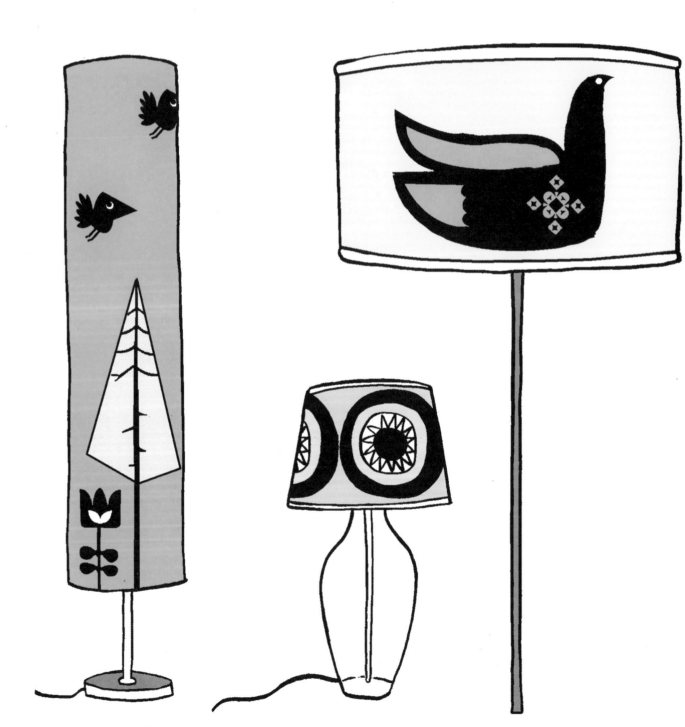

FreeStyle

Sketch out your ideas for
illuminating lampshades here.

Sparkling Shades

Creating your own designer lampshade couldn't be easier. Just follow these simple steps.

1 Use a sharp pencil and draw each design element on the lampshade. Don't worry if your lines are a little wobbly because that adds to the hand-drawn appeal.

2 Slowly add to the design in pencil until you are happy with it. Try not to press too hard with your pencil, because thick lines are harder to erase if you make a mistake.

3 Once you are happy with your pencil outline, you can paint it. This design uses two colors, but you can use more, if you prefer.

4 Use a fine brush to first paint on the lighter color. It's easier to paint the darker color last because it will cover any lighter areas where the paint overlaps.

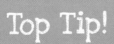

Top Tip!

Even a simple design of circles or stripes will look great.

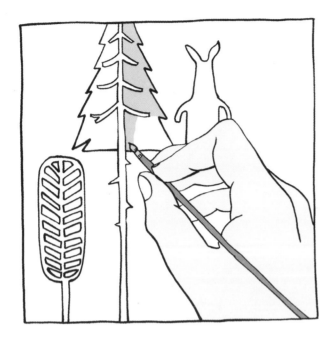

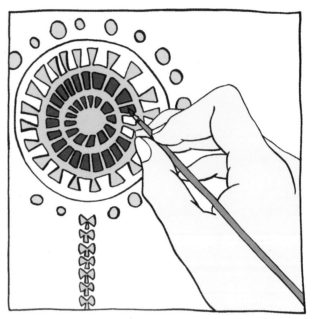

5 Use a medium brush to paint any larger areas in the lighter color. Turn on the light to see any areas that need a thicker coat of paint. Then let the lampshade dry.

6 Now use a fine brush to paint all the remaining dark areas. Take your time and try to make the edges meet as smoothly as possible. Go over any patchy areas, and then let dry.

Get some design inspiration from book illustrations.

7 Turn the light on and watch your
design light up the world!

Top Tip!

You can also use the
collage technique
on a lampshade.

Glossary

Abstract art
A style of art that is made up of lines, colors, and shapes instead of figures or objects from the real world.

Acetate
A type of plastic that is available in clear, thin, and flexible sheets, good for making reusable stencils.

Appliqué
A decorative design made by cutting pieces of one material and applying them to the surface of another.

Banksy
The name of the British graffiti artist and painter whose true identity is a closely guarded secret. His street art combines politics and dark humor with graffiti using a distinctive stenciling technique. It is featured on streets, walls, and bridges in cities all over the world.

Brayer
A small hand roller used to spread ink.

Collage
A style of art made by assembling pieces of paper and photographs to create a completely new image.

Craft knife
A single-blade sharp tool that can be used to cut through a variety of different materials.

Dressmaker's marking pencil
A type of pencil that can be used to temporarily mark fabric.

Duct tape

A cloth-backed, strong, and flexible type of adhesive tape.

Font

An alphabet with all the letters designed in the same style.

Fusible webbing

Sometimes called fusible inferfacing or simply fusible web, an artificial material that melts when heated (for example with an iron). When placed between two fabrics and heated, it acts like a glue, fusing the two pieces together.

Jagua temporary tattoo ink

A harmless body paint, similar to henna, that comes from the tropical fruit *Genipa americana*. Jagua ink has been used to create traditional body art in South America for hundreds of years. The effects last for a few weeks by staining the skin.

Linoleum

Often called lino, a type of hard-wearing flooring material. Similar in texture to vinyl, it is made from natural fibers and is easy to carve, making it a great alternative to wood when making printing blocks.

Linoleum cutter

A handy tool used for carving accurate details into linoleum. It is also perfect for carving pumpkins at Halloween.

Masking tape

A thin, easy-to-tear paper tape that you can buy in a variety of widths. Masking tape is easy to remove without leaving a sticky mark behind, which makes it perfect for art and craft activities.

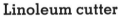

Motif

A distinctive object or shape that is repeated to create a pattern.

Polymer clay

A type of modeling clay available in various colors that is easy to shape and can be baked hard to create jewelry, ornaments, and models.

Retro

A trend or fashion that was popular in the past and is back in style again.

Stencil

A thin sheet of cardboard or plastic with a design cut into it. It is used to transfer the design to a surface beneath it by applying paint, ink, or dye through the cutout sections. The stencil can be reused to repeat the design.

Template

A sheet or block cut into a pattern and used as a guide to create an image.

Tracing paper

Semitransparent paper that can be used to transfer a design from one surface to another.

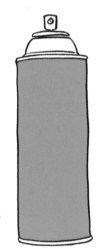

Vinyl covering

This durable flexible plastic can be purchased in sheets or rolls in a range of colors. The adhesive backing makes it easy to use for wall stickers and other projects.